CRIMCOMICS
ORIGINS OF CRIMINOLOGY

KRISTA S. GEHRING
WRITER

MICHAEL R. BATISTA
ARTIST

PATRICK M. POLLARD
INKER

CHERYL L. WALLACE
LETTERER

New York   Oxford
OXFORD UNIVERSITY PRESS

Dedication
To Mom,
Who took me to the library.
To Dad,
Who used to tell me bedtime stories.
To Natalee,
Who I am now writing the story of my life with.

—KRISTA S. GEHRING

To my Mom, Dad, and Sister,
for all their encouragement and support.
To my wife, Jeri, and my boys, Ash and Olly.
Thank you for your endless patience.

—MICHAEL R. BATISTA

FOREWORD

Growing up in the 1950s—a period generally considered to span the "golden" and "silver" ages of the comic book—I loved "my comics," gleefully thanking my mother whenever she would do me the special favor of purchasing the latest issue. These graphic depictions of superheroes and other interesting characters were useful diversions in an era when television carried only three major networks, computers and video games had yet to be invented, and most stimulating experiences could be found outside rather than inside one's house. I wondered whether in more modern times, comics had lost their adherents and been relegated to the dustbin of outmoded entertainment. Much to my surprise, the appeal of comic books has proven to be enduring. One source reports that in 2014, revenues from the sale of comics reached $935 million, including $100 million in digital sales. The leading comic book in 2014, *The Amazing Spider-Man*, is estimated to have sold 559,217 copies (see http://www.comichron.com/).

From what I understand, the comic book was originally a compilation of popular comic strips or "funnies" initially published in newspapers. Eventually, however, the comic became its own art form, conveying a coherent narrative. It was discovered that stories could be told by sequencing drawn pictures in one frame after another, with words interspersed to give voice to the characters. Due to their origin in the funnies, early comic books were intended to be humorous. Soon thereafter, stories broadened to include diverse subject matter that was not restricted to amusement. The first Superman comic book, for example, appeared in 1938, followed the next year by one featuring Batman.

My own tastes were eclectic. I enjoyed superheroes, with Superman being my favorite over Batman. But I found as well a measure of amusement in the comic called *Archie*, which featured Archie Andrews—a freckled-faced, red-haired, All-American teen—his friend Jughead, and his rival Reggie. I suspect I had a crush of sorts on the two attractive female characters, Betty and Veronica. My academic temperament, however, was manifested early on in the interest I also took in *Classic Comics*, a series in which each comic would tell the story of a classic book in literature. The first title in the series was *The Three Musketeers* (1941), followed by such issues as *Moby Dick*, *A Tale of Two Cities*, *Les Misérables*, and *Huckleberry Finn*. I must confess that my enjoyment of these comics was diminished by a tinge of guilt, a sense that I was cheating by not reading the original books. The reality was that unless assigned them in school, I would never have trudged through the full volumes. Comics were more fun—and taught me stories I would not have otherwise known.

This insight suggests that comic books might serve not only as a source of entertainment but also as an educational tool. In the teaching literature, comics are often touted as a useful way to lure struggling students, especially boys, to enjoy learning and to improve reading skills. But setting aside this potentially important function, reading comic books might be an invaluable means through which *knowledge is communicated and learned by all students*—whether struggling or talented, junior high school or college. To be sure, there is intrinsic value in reading a good book that is not easily measured by, say, multiple choice tests. Still, education often involves the narrow task of communicating subject-matter content. An implicit assumption is that traditional textbooks are the most legitimate way to transfer knowledge—and, by implication, that comic books are a trivial genre, better suited to supplying mindless stimulation that comes from following the exploits of superheroes and silly characters. Alas, the relative effectiveness of textbooks versus comic textbooks—called "graphic texts" (similar to "graphic novels")—cannot be settled by fiat. It is an empirical question as to which genre does a better job delivering knowledge to students.

In 2013, Jeremy Short, Brandon Randolph-Seng, and Aaron McKenny took up this issue in an academic article published in *Business Communication Quarterly* (vol. 76, no. 3, pp. 273–303). In a course on strategic management, students were assigned a graphic novel, *Atlas Black: The Complete Adventure*, as a way of illuminating key topics and constructs. A graphic novel is much like a lengthy comic book, except that it presents a more complex story typically aimed at a high school or adult audience. In a survey, the researchers found that senior undergraduate students agreed that use of *Atlas Black* facilitated the achievement of course objectives, increased learning engagement, and provided a comfortable learning experience. More instructive, Short and colleagues also conducted an experiment in which they compared learning outcomes for two groups of students: those who read an excerpt from the graphic novel versus those who read an excerpt from a standard management textbook. Based on a multivariate analysis, they reported that readers of the graphic novel either did as well (in the "recall and transfer" of knowledge) or better (in "verbatim recognition" of textbook materials) than readers of a traditional textbook.

Admittedly, one study, limited in scope and subject matter, does not establish that a graphic text, such as *CrimComics*, is a superior way to transmit knowledge to students. But at the very least, it suggests that the graphic portrayal of information in a comic book format has the potential to be a valuable supplement to traditional textbooks. Indeed, I fear that graphic texts may be the only way to communicate knowledge to many undergraduates. Reading texts undoubtedly improves learning, but the difficulty is in getting students actually to read anything. It appears that for a number of students, wading through a traditional textbook is seen as an onerous task to be undertaken mainly under threat of a looming examination.

Kylie Baier and colleagues probed this issue in a 2011 article published in the online journal, *American Reading Forum Annual Yearbook* (vol. 31). Using 395 participants drawn from two Midwestern universities, they found that "a staggering 62% of students spend an hour or less reading their assigned materials." About one in five students said that they did not complete the readings at all, and nearly nine in ten said that they could earn a C in the course without cracking the textbook (indeed, 63.8% thought an A or B was possible without reading). Less than a quarter stated that they completed assigned readings prior to class, whereas four in ten said that they did the readings only when studying for an examination. Again, assigning graphic texts may not solve this problem, but their distinctive format could reach some students turned off by traditional forms of course readings. It seems worth a try, if not an experimental evaluation!

In this regard, I found this first issue of *CrimComics* to be thoroughly engaging. My bias that comic books are inherently less serious than a regular academic text (especially if written by me!) was quickly dissipated. The quality of the writing by Krista Gehring and the artwork by Michael Batista soon had me so engrossed that I was anxious to turn page after page—even though, as a criminologist, I knew how the account would end. After the experience of reading this initial installment, I reflected on why I found the work so compelling. Two considerations came to mind.

First and foremost, similar to the comic books that I loved as a kid, Gehring and Batista's graphic text tells a story. Most traditional texts are compendiums of facts conveyed in page after page of dense writing. Please do not get me wrong: I write and like to read academic books, and believe that they are enormously valuable. But a key reason why the graphic text offers something novel is that it communicates knowledge in a distinctive way. I forget most facts that I learn, but I remember most stories. I do not think I am alone in this regard.

Second, illustrations are a neat way to conjure up a visual image that is absent from a text-only book. It is not just that a "picture is worth a thousand words." Rather, it is that well-crafted artwork creates a format in which the words used are placed within a visual context. In particular, clever writing allows the characters portrayed on the page to be given a voice and, in that way, to come "alive." The characters—whether Superman or Lombroso—are not only being talked about in the book but are talking themselves. Their conversation makes the text more like a television show—half documentary, half soap opera.

This focus on form should not, however, diminish the importance of quality content. Whether a text is traditional or graphic, it can be a good book or bad book. In the academic arena, a "good" book depends not only on presentation but also on getting the criminological facts correct. I am happy to report that *CrimComics* ultimately succeeds because the criminology being communicated is first rate.

In this issue, *CrimComics* tells what I would refer to as the "Story of the Two Cesares." I have always found it remarkable that the two most prominent figures in the origins of criminology were both named Cesare—Beccaria and Lombroso. I will not say too much and spoil the story to come. But I will share that each in his own way established a way of viewing crime—Beccaria with the Classic School and Lombroso with the Positivist School—that continues to shape theoretical criminology and crime-control policy to this day.

Let me conclude by reiterating my strong endorsement of *CrimComics*. Krista Gehring and Michael Batista have formed a fruitful partnership, combining scholarly and artistic expertise to create a groundbreaking work that promises to shape the communication and teaching of criminological knowledge well into the foreseeable future. Readers are about to embark on an unprecedented exploration of the ideas that have shaped modern thinking about crime. Having completed this trip already, I can attest that it is an exciting adventure well worth undertaking.

FRANCIS T. CULLEN
University of Cincinnati

PREFACE

The circumstances that would eventually produce *CrimComics* materialized over a decade ago. This project began when Mike and I were in the criminal justice master's program at Northeastern University in 2003. One night, some of the students went out and Mike confessed to the group that he really wanted to have his own comic book. I casually mentioned that I might have some stories that we could collaborate on, and the partnership was born. However, once we finished the program, I left Boston and returned to Colorado while Mike stayed on the East Coast.

While I pursued my doctoral degree at the University of Cincinnati, I taught undergraduate courses and found teaching criminological theory was difficult. The concepts were very abstract, and the students generally did not have much of an interest in the material. How could I "tell the story" of each theory if the current undergrad textbooks didn't do that? I started to do it in my lectures, but I wished I had something more. The current textbooks were either very dense and just listed the theories, paragraph after paragraph, or they were filled with a lot of material/activities/boxes that distracted from the material. Neither iteration of textbook really "told the story" of these theories. So what textbooks could I use and how could I make this material more interesting?

Then I got *the idea*. I called Mike and said, "Hey, what do you think about creating criminology comic books?" His immediate response was, "I think this was what we were meant to do." We put together some ideas regarding the issues and the scope of work, and thus the partnership with Oxford began.

As with any book project, *CrimComics* consumed much time and effort, perhaps more so than a traditional textbook. Thinking about theory—and, in particular, trying to design a work that best conveys the theories in a visual medium—is fun. Still, with busy lives, finding the space in one's day to carefully research, write, illustrate, ink, and letter the pages of this work was a source of some stress. We were fortunate, however, to have had an amazing amount of support during these times from family, friends, and Oxford University Press. We also want to acknowledge the talents of Pat Pollard and Cheryl Wallace. Pat's talent generated the inks for this issue that provided the unique look of the artwork, and Cheryl's flair for lettering allowed us to get our ideas across to the readers.

The support of these and so many other individuals has made creating *CrimComics* possible and a rewarding experience for us. We would like to thank the following reviewers: Donna Burnell, Alabama A&M University; Thomas J. Chuda, Bunker Hill Community College; Ellen G. Cohn, Florida International University; Barbara Allison Crowson, Norwich University; Anna Divita, University of North Carolina, Charlotte; Luigi Esposito, Barry University; Sara Evans, University of West Florida; Ashley K. Farmer, University of Delaware; Richard Inscore, Charleston Southern University; Deborah L. Johnson, Cameron University;

Paul Kaplan, San Diego State University; Allison Payne, Villanova University; Doshie Piper, University of the Incarnate Word; Patrick Polasek, Benedictine University; Tara N. Richards, University of Baltimore; Brenda Riley, Tarleton State University; Lisa Robinson, Central Carolina Community College; John Stogner, University of North Carolina, Charlotte; Angela Taylor, Fayetteville State University; and Allison Timbs, Campbellsville University. We hope that this and other issues of *CrimComics* will inspire in your students a passion to learn criminological theory.

Origins of Criminology

OUR THEORIES ABOUT WHY PEOPLE COMMIT CRIME INFLUENCE HOW SOCIETY DEALS WITH OFFENDERS.

THEREFORE, IN ANY STUDY OF CRIMINOLOGICAL THEORY, AN IMPORTANT UNDERLYING THEME SHOULD ALWAYS BE REMEMBERED:

IDEAS CAUSE REACTIONS.

OUR IDEAS, OR "THEORIES," ARE THE FOUNDATION OF PUBLIC POLICIES. THEY ARE THE BASIS OF LAWS AND CRIMINAL JUSTICE AGENCIES' PHILOSOPHIES.

RIGHT NOW, ANY MAJOR PUBLIC POLICY REGARDING CRIME MAKES FUNDAMENTAL ASSUMPTIONS ABOUT HUMAN BEHAVIOR. THESE ASSUMPTIONS TEND TO CHANGE OVER TIME.

WHAT WAS ONCE BELIEVED TO BE THE CAUSE OF CRIMINAL BEHAVIOR IN THE PAST IS PERHAPS NO LONGER RELEVANT OR APPLICABLE IN THE PRESENT.

THAT IS, THE SAME THEORY HAS NOT GUIDED EVERY REACTION TO CRIME THROUGHOUT THE AGES.

WHAT IS COMMON PRACTICE TODAY WASN'T DONE SEVERAL DECADES AGO.

SO HOW DID WE GET TO WHERE WE ARE NOW?

LET'S TAKE A LOOK AT THE ORIGINS OF CRIMINOLOGY...

FOR CENTURIES, THE PREVAILING IDEOLOGY THAT SHAPED IDEAS ABOUT HUMAN BEHAVIOR EMPHASIZED RELIGION, BLIND FAITH, AND SUPERSTITION.

BECAUSE OF THIS, ORGANIZED RELIGIONS WERE POWERFUL ENTITIES THAT WERE ABLE TO OUTLINE THE EXPECTATIONS OF THEIR FOLLOWERS BASED ON THEIR BELIEF IN A SUPREME BEING.

ONE OF THE MOST WELL-KNOWN TEXTS FOR THESE EXPECTATIONS IS THE BIBLE, A WORK THAT DESCRIBES VARIOUS SOCIAL AND MORAL LAWS HUMANS SHOULD FOLLOW...

...AND THE PUNISHMENTS TO METE OUT IF THEY DID NOT FOLLOW THESE RULES.

THESE PUNISHMENTS WERE OFTEN BASED IN THE NOTION OF AN "EYE FOR AN EYE" (DEUTERONOMY 19:21)

SINCE THESE RULES WERE
SUPPOSEDLY GIVEN TO HUMANS
BY A DIVINE BEING, THOSE WHO
WENT AGAINST THESE RULES
WERE ASSUMED TO BE IN ALLIANCE
WITH SATAN AND HIS MINIONS.

FOR CENTURIES HUMANS USED
THIS AS AN EXPLANATION OF
CRIMINAL BEHAVIOR. FOR MANY,
SIN AND CRIMINAL BEHAVIOR WERE
ONE AND THE SAME.

THIS WAS REFERRED TO AS **SPIRITUALISM**.

THIS BELIEF SYSTEM PROPOSED THAT
INDIVIDUALS COMMITTED CRIME
BECAUSE THEY WERE EVIL OR
POSSESSED BY SPIRITS OR DEMONS.

CRIMINALS ENGAGED IN CRIME BECAUSE
"THE DEVIL MADE THEM DO IT."

PUNISHMENTS WERE MEANT TO RID THE COMMUNITY OF DEMONS AND OTHER EVIL SPIRITS.

THE PAIN INFLICTED BY CORPOREAL PUNISHMENTS WAS INTENDED TO DRIVE OUT THE DEMON OR TO EXTRACT CONFESSIONS OF THE PERSON'S ALLEGIANCE WITH THE DEVIL.

CAPITAL PUNISHMENT WAS MEANT TO KILL NOT ONLY THE PERSON, BUT THE DEMON THAT RESIDED IN HIM.

EVIDENCE OF THIS EXISTS THROUGHOUT HISTORY: MANY SOCIETIES HAVE EXECUTED THOUSANDS OF INDIVIDUALS BELIEVED TO BE WITCHES OR POSSESSED BY DEMONS.

IN THE SEVENTEENTH AND EIGHTEENTH CENTURIES, A PHILOSOPHICAL, INTELLECTUAL, AND CULTURAL MOVEMENT EMERGED IN EUROPE.

THE IDEAS THAT EMERGED DURING THIS MOVEMENT STRESSED REASON, LOGIC, AND CRITICISM.

SUPPORTERS OF THIS MOVEMENT PROPOSED THAT FREE WILL AND RATIONAL THOUGHT WERE THE BASIS OF HUMAN BEHAVIOR.

THIS WAS REFERRED TO AS *"THE ENLIGHTENMENT"* OR THE "AGE OF REASON."

MILAN, ITALY, 1763.

AS A YOUNG ADULT, *CESARE BECCARIA* READ FRENCH AND ENGLISH PHILOSOPHERS AND WROTE ESSAYS ON VARIOUS TOPICS PERTAINING TO ENLIGHTENMENT ISSUES.

HE OFTEN DISCUSSED HIS IDEAS WITH HIS FRIENDS.

LONDON, ENGLAND, 1785.

CESARE BECCARIA WAS NOT THE ONLY PERSON TO BELIEVE THAT PUNISHMENT SHOULD BE A DETERRENT.

SAMUEL, YOU OLD COOT! HOW ARE YOU MY BROTHER?

JEREMY BENTHAM, AN ENGLISH JURIST, PHILOSOPHER, AND SOCIAL REFORMER, ALSO HAD IDEAS ABOUT HOW PUNISHMENT SHOULD AFFECT SOCIETY.

NOT ONLY WAS HE INFLUENCED BY ENLIGHTENMENT IDEAS, BUT HE LIVED DURING A TIME OF GREAT SOCIAL AND POLITICAL UNREST.

AT THIS TIME, ENGLAND WAS EXPERIENCING ITS INDUSTRIAL REVOLUTION AS WELL AS THE RISE OF THE MIDDLE CLASS. GLOBALLY, FRANCE AND AMERICA WERE INVOLVED IN REVOLUTIONS.

THESE EVENTS INSPIRED HIS PERSONAL REVELATIONS REGARDING HUMAN NATURE AND PUNISHMENT.

FINE, JEREMY. I CAN SEE YOU ARE IN GOOD SPIRITS TODAY. TO WHAT CAUSE?

I'VE BEEN THINKING, SAMUEL. THINKING, THINKING!

OH DEAR. NO GOOD CAN COME FROM THAT.

NONSENSE! I KNOW YOU SAY THAT IN JEST!

I HAVE BEEN PONDERING HUMAN NATURE AND HOW THIS RELATES TO PUNISHMENT, SAMUEL.

UPON HIS DEATH, BENTHAM WILLED HIS BODY TO HIS FRIEND DR. SOUTHWOOD SMITH, TO BE THE SUBJECT OF A DISSECTION AND ANATOMY LECTURE.

AFTER THE DISSECTION, BENTHAM REQUESTED THAT HIS BODY BE PRESERVED, DRESSED IN HIS CLOTHES, AND SEATED IN A CHAIR IN A CABINET FOR OTHERS TO OBSERVE.

THE SEATED FIGURE OF JEREMY BENTHAM STILL SITS AT THE UNIVERSITY COLLEGE IN LONDON.

HIS BODY HAS ATTENDED MANY FACULTY AND COUNCIL MEETINGS.

IT IS ALWAYS RECORDED THAT HE IS "PRESENT, BUT NOT VOTING."

THE ENLIGHTENMENT AND BECCARIA AND BENTHAM'S WRITINGS USHERED IN WHAT IS KNOWN AS THE *CLASSICAL SCHOOL* OF CRIMINOLOGY.

THIS LINE OF THINKING PROPOSED THAT ALL MEN HAD THE ABILITY TO EXERCISE *FREE WILL*. THEY HAD A CHOICE REGARDING THEIR BEHAVIORS.

CLASSICAL THEORY ASSUMES THAT HUMAN BEINGS ARE HEDONISTIC; THAT IS, THEY SEEK PLEASURE AND AVOID PAIN. THE CHOICES THEY MAKE ARE FUELED BY THIS ASSUMPTION.

A CERTAIN AMOUNT OF PLEASURE IS DERIVED FROM ENGAGING IN CRIMINAL BEHAVIOR. THEREFORE, FEAR OF PUNISHMENT SHOULD DETER THIS BEHAVIOR.

THAT IS, FEAR OF PUNISHMENT WILL IMPACT WHETHER OR NOT A PERSON CHOOSES TO COMMIT CRIME.

CONVENIENCE STORE

asymmetry of the face

low, sloping forehead

high cheek bones

ears of unusual size

fleshy lips

excessive dimensions
of the jaw

excessive length
of arms

tattoos

THESE WERE THE SORTS OF *STIGMATA*
LOMBROSO BELIEVED EVIDENCED
THE CRIMINALS' ATAVISTIC STATE.

LOMBROSO'S FINDINGS WERE
PUBLISHED IN HIS WORK
L'UOMO DELINQUENTE (1876)
OR "THE CRIMINAL MAN."

ALTHOUGH LOMBROSO'S THEORIES ABOUT THE CAUSES OF CRIMINAL BEHAVIOR HAVE LONG BEEN ABANDONED, HE IS REFERRED TO AS THE "FATHER OF CRIMINOLOGY."

HIS WORK WAS AN EXAMPLE OF ANOTHER SCHOOL OF CRIMINOLOGICAL THOUGHT.

UNLIKE THE CLASSICAL SCHOOL'S EMPHASIS ON RATIONAL THOUGHT AND FREE WILL, THE *POSITIVIST SCHOOL* STRESSED A SEARCH FOR SCIENTIFIC FACTS THAT CRIME WAS CAUSED BY MULTIPLE FACTORS.

POSITIVISM WAS A SCIENTIFIC APPROACH. IT REJECTED METAPHYSICAL EXPLANATIONS OF PHENOMENA. ITS FOCUS WAS WHAT COULD BE OBSERVED AND MEASURED.

AS INDICATED HERE, LOMBROSO WANTED SCIENTIFIC PROOF THAT CRIME WAS CAUSED BY FEATURES WITHIN THE INDIVIDUAL.

MUCH THEORETICAL RESEARCH TODAY RELIES ON A POSITIVISTIC APPROACH.

THAT IS, SCHOLARS LOOK FOR QUANTITATIVE, OR EMPIRICAL, EVIDENCE TO SUPPORT A PARTICULAR THEORY.

THE THEORIES PRESENTED IN THIS ISSUE WERE A SIGN OF THE TIMES-- THEY DID NOT APPEAR IN A VACUUM AND ARE THEREFORE NOT EXEMPT FROM THE SOCIO-HISTORICAL CONTEXT IN WHICH THEY WERE CREATED.

BECCARIA'S IDEAS WERE INFLUENCED BY THE ENLIGHTENMENT MOVEMENT...

...WHILE LOMBROSO WAS A FOLLOWER OF DARWIN'S THEORY OF EVOLUTION.

CRIMCOMICS

INDEED, COMPONENTS OF THESE THEORIES HAVE PREVAILED OVER TIME AND HAVE INFLUENCED MODERN-DAY THINKING ABOUT CRIMINAL BEHAVIOR.

THIS ISSUE BEGAN WITH A DISCUSSION OF THE PREVAILING PERSPECTIVES OF CRIMINAL BEHAVIOR THROUGHOUT MOST OF HUMAN HISTORY, WHICH WERE SUPERNATURAL AND/OR RELIGIOUS-BASED THEORIES. HOWEVER, WHEN THE ENLIGHTENMENT MOVEMENT EMERGED IN THE 17TH AND 18TH CENTURIES, A MORE RATIONAL DISCUSSION ABOUT HUMAN BEHAVIOR INFLUENCED IDEAS REGARDING LEGAL AND PENAL REFORMS. DURING THIS TIME, THE CLASSICAL SCHOOL OF CRIMINOLOGICAL THOUGHT BECAME THE DOMINANT PHILOSOPHY, WITH CESARE BECCARIA AND JEREMY BENTHAM BEING MAJOR PROPONENTS OF THESE IDEAS. THE MAIN PROPOSITION OF THIS SCHOOL OF THOUGHT IS THAT OFFENDERS ARE RATIONAL BEINGS, HAVE FREE WILL, AND CHOOSE TO COMMIT CRIME BASED ON THE PERCEIVED RISK OF GETTING CAUGHT AND/OR BEING PUNISHED. PUNISHMENT SHOULD HAVE SOME UTILITY BEYOND THAT OF MERE VENGEANCE--IT SHOULD ALSO DETER.

THIS ISSUE ALSO DISCUSSED THE EMERGENCE OF THE POSITIVIST SCHOOL OF CRIMINOLOGY, WHICH WAS VERY DIFFERENT FROM THE PREVAILING CLASSICAL SCHOOL PARADIGM. WHILE THE CLASSICAL SCHOOL PROPOSED FREE WILL AND INDIVIDUAL CHOICE WERE INVOLVED IN CRIMINAL BEHAVIOR, THE POSITIVIST SCHOOL DID NOT BELIEVE THEY WERE INVOLVED AT ALL. ON THE CONTRARY, CRIMINAL BEHAVIOR WAS CAUSED BY FACTORS THAT WERE BEYOND THE INDIVIDUAL'S CONTROL. WITH THE ADVENT OF DARWIN'S THEORY OF EVOLUTION, THIS USHERED IN NEW WAYS OF THEORIZING ABOUT CRIMINAL BEHAVIOR. THE MOST NOTABLE CRIMINOLOGIST WHO WAS INFLUENCED BY THESE IDEAS WAS CESARE LOMBROSO, ALSO KNOWN AS THE FATHER OF CRIMINOLOGY. HE PROPOSED THAT CRIMINALS WERE EVOLUTIONARILY INFERIOR TO NON-CRIMINALS AND THIS WAS EVIDENCED BY CERTAIN PHYSICAL CHARACTERISTICS. HIS IDEAS SUPPORTED THE NOTION THAT CRIMINALS WERE BORN, NOT MADE.

Key Terms

Spiritualism

The Enlightenment

Cesare Beccaria

Jeremy Bentham

Utilitarianism

Classical School

Free Will

Determinism

Charles Darwin

Cesare Lombroso

Stigmata

Atavism

Criminal Anthropology

Positivist School

Positivism

Discussion Questions

How do pre-Enlightenment perspectives of crime differ from those developed during the Enlightenment era?

Which concepts put forth by Cesare Beccaria do you find the most practical? The least practical?

What modern-day criminal justice policies do you think are based upon the ideas proposed by Beccaria and/or Bentham?

What characteristics distinguish the Positivist School from the Classical School regarding crime and criminals? Which of these schools of thought do you lean more toward when you think about crime and why?

List some of the factors Lombroso said distinguish "born criminals" from others. How would one go about providing a good test of Lombroso's theory?

What policy recommendations might someone who believes in Lombroso's theory advocate for controlling crime?

Suggested Readings

Beccaria, C. (1764). *An essay on crimes and punishments*. Retrieved from
  http://oll.libertyfund.org/titles/2193.

Bentham, J. (1780). *An introduction to the principles and morals of legislation*. Retrieved
  from http://oll.libertyfund.org/titles/278.

Cullen, F.T., Agnew, R., & Wilcox, P. (2014). *Criminological theory: Past to present, 5th
  edition*. New York: Oxford University Press.

Darwin, C. (1859/2003). *The origin of the species*. New York: Signet Publishing.

Darwin, C. (1871/2004). *The descent of man*. London: Penguin Classics.

Lilly, J.R., Cullen, F.T., and Ball, R. (2011). *Criminological theory: Context and
  consequences*. Los Angeles: Sage Publications.

Lombroso, C. (1876/2006). *Criminal man*. Durham, NC: Duke University Press Books.

Lombroso, C. (2010). *The female offender*. Charleston, SC: Nabu Press.

Rafter, N. (1997). *Creating born criminals*. Urbana: University of Illinois Press.